THE ICE PUNCH

By Brian Duncan

Copyright © 2020 by Brian Duncan

All rights reserved. No part of this publication may be reproduced, distributed or transmitted in any form or by any means, including photocopying, recording or other electronic or mechanical methods, without prior written permission of the author.

While the author has made every reasonable effort to trace the copyright owners for any or all of the photographs in this book, there may be some omissions of credits, for which I apologise.

First edition 2020.

Cover design: Radoslav Metodiev

Book design, layout and editing by Brian Duncan

Dedications:

For Dai Bowen and Leslie Williams, to the families of both boys, and to all the lost souls that went down with the Titanic.

For my wife Michelle, and our two sons, Braiden and Callen.

Excerpt - The Loss Of The *Titanic*.

A gallant ship set sail one day, with its monstrous living freight.

A palace grand, a town indeed for ease it had no mate.

Within ship's walls such luxury, no eye had ever seen,

A nest for bride and bridegroom more fitting ne'er had been.

Friends and relations by the score had gathered there to wave,

A last "goodbye," mayhap to Duke, mayhap to seaman brave.

They all just clustered at the side to snatch a farewell look,

For tho it now seemed fair and bright, none knows what's in the book.

And so they parted, rich and poor, no difference in their grief,

For tears will run down the cheeks of all, when the last look is so brief.

Parting at all times makes one sad, but if they had only known,

'Twas a terrible, awful last farewell - for the sea was to claim its own. -

Madge Duckworth

Contents

INTRODUCTION	6
CHAPTER 1: Ready To Manifest	8
CHAPTER 2: Off The Canvas	23
CHAPTER 3: The Calling	42
CHAPTER 4: The Fatal Blow	62
SOURCES & ACKNOWLEDGEMENTS	86

INTRODUCTION

My two young sons were obsessed with James Cameron's blockbuster movie *Titanic* and had found their way onto Youtube on our television. They had clicked on a documentary about her victims, and after a few minutes two boxers from Wales were mentioned, David John Bowen and Leslie Williams. I remember thinking I had never heard of them before. "How did they get on the *Titanic*? What happened to them? What were their plans for America?" My interest was up. That same night I scoured through some old newspaper articles from the time and their names appeared, although very sparingly, and with different tales about the two lads. It was clear from the very beginning this was going to be an arduous task and would take a lot of time to sort out fact from fiction.

None of what I initially found was making much sense so I contacted some friends, boxing and *Titanic* historians/authors. It was a very interesting story, one that should be told, and after some discussion, one that I should tell myself. Initially I had reservations as I hadn't tackled a book before and the research needed was going to mean long days and lonely nights, with little time for anything else. After toing and froing with myself, I had decided. Afterall, we have all heard of the *Titanic*, a beautiful leviathan, made up of steel and iron and thousands of rivets. For Bowen and Williams, they were real people with families and friends and expected opponents.

    Through social media and being active around boxing history, I pulled on my friendships with individuals and groups of brilliant researchers. From picking their brains, contacting Universities and Libraries and digging through archived paperwork, I was able to gather as much information as was out there. Their story was ready to be told. During writing, and as a rare break, I would spend an hour or two putting together a model *Titanic*. Constructing it piece by piece, I couldn't help think I was doing the same thing in attempting to tell the story of the two boys from the Rhondda Valley.

CHAPTER 1: Ready To Manifest

At the turn of the twentieth century, any good American boxer could have gone over to the UK and whipped all of their fighters one after another, from light to heavyweight. It was labelled a pugilistic "dead one." Things were changing. The stay-at-home fighters were being left a long way behind as on their return from invading America, the best little battlers in the Kingdom flashed large quantities of greenback and were bringing out much advanced American boxing methods. They had roused a new interest in the game.

Hoosier native Kid McCoy's junketing trips to England were a distant memory, and no longer the jokes of the time. He did, however, show the importance of getting the coin. The islanders were being viewed as easy marks by club managers until McCoy was booked to box at Wonderland, London, where he was to be given the usual trimming. McCoy dealt with three opponents in the same night, beating David Barry, Jack Scales and Sandy Ferguson. A mountainous feat no doubt, but given he had been in the ring with legendary fighters such as Joe Choynski, Tommy Ryan, Tom Sharkey and James J Corbett, nobody's eyebrows were raised. After he returned to his dressing room, he had an inkling that something was amiss in the box office and that by the time he arrived to count up, his end would have shrunken to peanut proportions. Thinking quickly and before getting the usual rub down, he slipped into his trousers, hat and overcoat and made his way to the box office. On entering, one unfortunate lad was sitting counting up. McCoy grabbed what he felt was his share and darted through the side door of Wonderland into the reception room where the matches were made, through another side door into the street and into a waiting car. Within seconds he was tearing for the train. "E was beastly sharp" complained a witness, "E didn't leave enough to pay the preliminary bouts."

"The Fearless" Owen Moran had fought in America in 1905 and he was back in the UK and was matched with Cockney Cohen, regarded at the time as one of the best boxers in England. The much anticipated fight took place on the 22nd Feb 1906, at the Liverpool Gymnastic Club, for a purse of £750 and a side bet of £500. Although the lads were to box at 118lbs, Cohen towered over Moran with a 4inch height advantage.

Moran was not phased, and employing the American way, dispatched Cohen via a fourth round knockout. Moran agreed to a re-match in Glasgow and on the night of the 23rd March 1906, he won in even quicker fashion, this time obliterating Cohen in three. Across the pond, Moran was now considered a genuine threat to anyone of similar size.

The heavyweight class had a developing story in Gunner Moir that was grabbing the imagination of the fight fans. Some old timers were comparing Moir to Jem Mace and Charlie Mitchell, while the Sportsman said that Moir was the best heavyweight England had produced since Charlie Mitchell's time. Owen Moran himself said, "Moir can whip any man in the world except Jeffries. He is big and strong. He wrestled with Hackenschmidt and developed a lot of strength, but he wont wrestle anymore. He spends all of his time boxing and training for speed. He was slow at the start, but now he is quite fast and he boxes just like an American. He is a clever big man, and he can hit hard enough to knock anybody out." Moir was after the coveted heavyweight championship of the world and got his chance when Tommy Burns made the journey over to England to square off against him at The National Sporting Club in Covent Garden, London. Burns was favoured to win although the press were less than complimentary. "Though we have little doubt that Tommy will be able to fix the Englishman's clock a la Bill Squires, it seems too bad that a more representative American could not have made the journey." Burns was said to be no match for Jeffries who, even with one arm tied behind his back, could "lick him." Moir may have been wishing it was Burns who had one arm tied behind his back this night as Burns controlled the fight, knocking the much bigger Moir down several times before finishing the fight in round ten of a scheduled twenty. Moir had done his bit in elevating the interest in the glove game on the Island, however his career after this loss would never be the same.

Back down the weights, great rivalries were emerging. Owen Moran and the legendary Abe Attell accepted terms of promoter Jimmy Coffroth of San Francisco to box in Colma, New Years day 1908 for a $6000 purse, with the privilege of taking sixty percent instead. The aforementioned Jim Jeffries refereed the twenty five round contest to a draw. Welsh wonder "Peerless" Jim Driscoll, a previous rival and opponent of Moran was after the winner and had travelled to America with $5400 belonging to members of the National Sporting Club of London, who were willing to put up that amount that he could beat any featherweight in the world. Driscoll was so good that his backers said he practically chased Owen Moran out of England. The press in America were not so sure. "It would be fine indeed, if when Driscoll arrives here, he should find that the 'chased' Moran was already ahead of him and had defeated the American title holder, Abe Attell. Moran will have to go some to make such a surprise possible, but if he does, Driscoll will find himself with a fight on his hands."

Attell twice risked his title in battles with Moran with the second bout in San Francisco also being scored a draw over twenty three rounds. Attell immediately went out of his weight class to tackle another travelling fighter, the "Welsh Wizard" Freddie Welsh. Welsh easily disposed of Attell, outpointing him over fifteen rounds. Welsh had been fighting some of the greatest pound for pound fighters around, including the brilliant Packey McFarland. They had met twice before, firstly in Milwaukee at the Milwaukee Boxing Club, where Packey was given the decision. Hisses and jeers rang aloud when Welsh did not get the verdict as it was said he "jabbed Packey from stern to stern and from start to finish and the worst he should have received was a draw." Only the Chicagoan and the Chicago crowd believed Packey had done enough to win. In the rematch, they battled out a draw over the longer twenty five rounds at Jeffries Arena, Vernon. Promoter Jimmy Coffroth was after a third 'go' after Welsh's latest showing against Attell. Welsh was a very popular fighter out west and he and Packey could draw a big house. The fans, and Cofforth, would get their wish, but would have to be patient as the fight was delayed.

Meanwhile "Peerless" Jim was defeating everyone he faced. In with Johnny Marto, the clever New York lightweight, Driscoll gave away around 10lbs in weight. The fight took place in Marto's backyard at the Fairmont A.C, Bronx, New York. Marto would become another fighter bamboozled by Driscoll's wonderful cleverness and at times was made to look foolish. Driscoll was now anxious to fight Abe Attell and they were eventually matched to fight on the 19th Feb 1909. Driscoll defeated Attell at The National A.C, New York, displaying another fine showing of ring craft and guile to win comfortably on points. By now, Charles J Harvey, manager of both Jim Driscoll and Owen Moran, had his say on the campaigning trio of Attell, Driscoll and Moran. "Abe Attell, instead of talking about the recent bout with Driscoll and making bluffs about $15,000 side bets in the event of another mill, should not lose sight of the fact that Owen Moran stands ready to make a match with the American featherweight champion, and allow the latter to name the conditions. Moran will fight Attell at any of the local clubs, the National and Fairmount preferred, ten rounds, as soon as Attell is ready to talk business. Attell talks about how he can whip Driscoll for the featherweight championship of the world, but he has never beaten Moran as yet." Back home, the performances of Driscoll and Welsh were inspiring a new breed of fighter. Around this time, early 1910, two names started to appear, that of Leslie Williams and David 'Dai' Bowen.

Williams was born Leslie Williams in the summer of 1888. His birth is recorded in quarter three of that year and his name is listed in the register covering the months of July, August and September. He first appears as a two year old in the 1891 census of England, Wales and Scotland as living at 4 Fernley Terrace along with ten other occupants. Among them were his mother Elizabeth Williams and six siblings, that being three brothers and three sisters. Leslie was the youngest boy, next was Harold who was four years old, Lewis was eight years old and Charles the eldest at sixteen. He had an infant baby sister Edith, with Margaret being six years of age and Elizabeth ten. Two boarders, Evan

Morris and Charles Irwen stayed with them and a visitor named David Rees made up the numbers. Leslie's birth home is sometimes incorrectly listed as Eleanor Street as they appear living there in the next census of 1901, however he was in fact born and spent his early years at Fernley Terrace. By the age of twelve Leslie was listed as an Apprentice Boiler Maker living at number 19 Eleanor Street. Even at this young and tender age, he was learning how tough he had to be to survive. Working hard jobs in hard environments with older men would mould him into a rough and respected fighter in the ring.

In early 1910 Leslie married his girlfriend Lily Thomas and their coupling appeared in the register of England and Wales Marriages of quarter two, covering April, May and June. One year later and the census of 1911 shows the young family living in Tonypandy, at 59 Primrose Street. Leslie was now head of the household and working as a Blacksmith Striker, and still only twenty two years old. He and Lily had moved into a new home, and along with Lily's mother Mary Jane who was living with them, they had welcomed a son, Leslie James Williams. Almost exactly one year later Leslie would be heading to America, leaving his family behind, and his expectant wife Lily, who was celebrating the upcoming arrival of their second child.

Born David John Bowen in the third quarter of 1891, 'Dai' was three years Leslie's junior. His birth appears in the register for July, August and September of that year. At the time of the 1901 census Dai is shown to be living with his widowed mother Leah Bowen and three siblings at 36 Baglan Street. Stephen was the youngest at seven years old, Dai is next listed as being ten although this was incorrect and he was actually nine at this time, James was the eldest brother at twenty two years old and his sister Maggie was thirteen years of age. By 1911 the Bowen family had moved three houses up in the same street and there were some changes to the dynamics in the family. Now at 42 Baglan Street, Dai was listed as nineteen years old, the age being corrected since the last census, single, and working as a Coal Miner Hewer. His younger brother Stephen had moved with them and his mother Leah had married Morris Owens and was now listed as Leah Owens. With Maggie and James away, this left the four of them together. Dai was the eldest of the children remaining and always felt it was his duty to protect his mother, working honestly and unselfishly to bring money and food into the household.

Both Leslie and Dai had been in and around gyms and primarily boxing throughout their youth and both had shown early signs of promise. It wouldn't take long before they were catching the eye. Although the press coverage in Wales was restricted, mainly due to a fierce backlash in some quarters against boxing, for Williams and Bowen this did nothing to deter them from pursuing a life in the ring. Williams

> LESS WILLIAMS (Tonypandy) will Box the following Boxers (15 or 20 rounds): Basham (Newport), Evans (Swansea), Badger O'Brien (Cardiff), C. Webber (Pontypridd).—Reply through "Evening Express." YOUNG J. L. SULLIVAN (Ireland) will Box Dai Peters 15 or 20 rounds, or anybody else at middleweight.

Leslie Williams keen to get in the ring, 17th Jan 1910

was eager to fight, and fight anyone. "Reply through the Evening Express" was the call as Williams offered to box Basham of Newport, Evans of Swansea, Badger O'Brien of Cardiff and C. Webber of Pontypridd, over fifteen or twenty rounds. He then went on to appear at

The Park-Hall in Cardiff for the twentieth annual Assault-at-Arms in aid of Nazareth House. "Champions Of The Ring" was the headline as Williams performed alongside Driscoll and Welsh. Packey McFarland was also booked to fight but as the crowd filled the building anxiously waiting to clap eyes on him, it was announced he had missed his train and on this occasion would be unable to attend.

Over the two nights of Monday 14th and Tuesday 15th March, 1910, a host of exciting boxers participated in some fine exhibition bouts. "Digger" Stanley, the English bantamweight champion and Johnny Curran, the Irish bantamweight champion were popular among the crowd, along with the tricky Wally Packard who upset the odds by knocking out Ernie Hooper of Cardiff, himself vying to become the English amatuer lightweight champion. Fred Dyer and "Young" Basham renewed old rivalries and there was a hard fought scrap between Eddie Carsey and Salam Sullivan. Other attractions at the event aside from boxing were the Royal Welsh Male Choir led by Mr. Thomas, the Saviours gymnastic team, the Cardiff Post-Office Band conducted by Mr. T. Sansom, and a comical encounter as councillor Peter Wright got in the ring for a ten minute wrestling bout with Bob Berry, the current holder of the Lonsdale belt for wrestling.

The boxing matches were the main draw, however, and Williams was in with future opponent Munro Grainger, Freddie Welsh had a "lively set-to" with Fred Delaney, while Jim Driscoll and former world champion Joe Bowker were forced to give an "encore" after their efforts over three rounds. The success of the event was said to be the greatest in its twenty year existence. "Probably at no other meeting of the kind in the British Isles could so excellent a programme be got together, nor yet could so enthusiastic a body of sportsmen be collected to give their time and money so freely as does that of the committee of the gathering under question. The result is that year by year all the best talent of the kingdom is available for the Park-Hall display, and boxers make all sorts of sacrifices to enable them to be present at the great annual gathering."

Dai Bowen was no different. The Millfield Athletic Club in Pontypridd was advertising the bout between Bowen and Bob Roberts of Treorchy as a "Grand 20 Round Boxing Contest." Scheduled for Saturday 2nd April 1910, they would box for £25 a-side and a £40 purse. The doors opened at 7:15pm, with the admission fee's set at 2s, 3s and

5s. Leading up to Dai's fight, a competition was held between boxers at 8st 4lb and 9st, with the winner taking home a silver cup and the runner up a silver medal, with anyone wanting to witness the bouts paying an extra 1 shilling. As Bowen and Roberts worked up a sweat and made their way to the ring amidst loud cheers, everyone was expecting a

> MILLFIELD ATHLETIC CLUB.
> SATURDAY, APRIL 2nd, 1910.
> Grand 20 Round Boxing Contest between
> BOB ROBERTS (Treorchy) and
> D. J. BOWEN (Treherbert),
> For £25 a-side and £40 purse. Stakeholders and Referee, "Sporting Life."
> Also 8st. 4lb. and 9st. COMPETITIONS. Winners, Silver Cup; Runners-up, Silver Medals.—Entries 1s. each to be sent to Secretary, Millfield Athletic Club, Pontypridd. Doors Open 7.15 p.m. First Bout 8 p.m.
> Admission, 5s., 3s., and 2s.

Dai's match with Bob Roberts was making headlines

closely fought fight. Roberts started swiftly in the first round, being the aggressor and looking for an early stoppage as Bowen sized up his opponent. As the round progressed, Bowen started to shine and showed to be the stronger man, soon making up the leeway. In the second round, Bowen changed his game and took the fight to his opponent, knocking

Roberts down with a heavy blow early on. As Roberts rose, Bowen unleashed a flurry of hard punches, flooring him a further two times and ending the fight in spectacular fashion.

It was performances like these that drew the boxing eyes to Dai and the following month, on Tuesday 17th May 1910, he appeared by invitation from Mr Dan Armstrong at a special boxing matinee at The Empire, Tonypandy with middleweight champion Tom Thomas. Commencing at 11:20am, there would be a ball punching display where Thomas would showcase his frightening knockout power, followed by a ball punching competition for local lads. Two six-round contests followed, with Bowen honing his skills against Trealaw lad Gordon Hughes before Mose Martin (Penygraig) battled Edgar Phillips (Williamstown). Tom Thomas would end the night with an exhibition fight against Tiger Smith. The increasing popularity of Bowen and Williams was becoming hard to ignore, owing to their willingness and gameness to fight, as well as scrapping alongside such luminaries as Driscoll, Welsh and Thomas. Although both were relatively inexperienced and still developing, they had garnered such a following that the next time both would appear, they would be headlining their respective events.

CHAPTER 2: Off The Canvas

Leslie Williams was up first. It was a Monday evening on the 4th July 1910. The Millfield A.C, the previous hunting ground of Dai Bowen, was filling up with eager fistic fans. Ringside seats were reserved for 5s and the admission prices had been set for 1s, 2s and 3s. The doors opened at 7:30pm and the crowd were entertained with two six-round contests, followed by the big fight at around 9pm between Williams and Ike Young Bradley, the

> **BOXING.**
> **MILLFIELD ATHLETIC CLUB, PONTYPRIDD.**
> MONDAY NEXT, JULY 4th, 1910.
> **GRAND TWENTY-ROUND CONTEST,**
> For £20 aside and £40 Purse,
> between
> IKE BRADLEY, Liverpool (5st. 4lb. Champion North of England), and
> LES WILLIAMS, Tonypandy (5st. 5lb. Champion South Wales).
> Stakeholders, "Evening Express," who also appoint Referee.
> ALSO TWO OTHER SIX-ROUND CONTESTS.
> Doors open 7.45 p.m. Big Contest 9 p.m.
> Admission—1s., 2s., 3s. Reserved Ringside Seats, 5s.

Leslie takes on the dangerous Ike Bradley

current North of England champion and one of the most durable and game fighters around. Bradley was a big fan favourite with a style to excite even the most equable spectator, and for Leslie this was a big step up in class in opponent. It was agreed they would be fighting for £20 a-side and a £40 purse. The stakeholders of the event were the Evening Express and they appointed Mr Harry Wells of Cardiff as referee. After the earlier bouts, the fans were ready for the twenty round main event, and they would not be disappointed. Round after round both lads tore into each other without dithering. Bradley was the more experienced and the following year he would be fighting for a title, but on this night there was nothing he could do as Williams was the better fighter, the harder to hit and was ahead in almost all aspects of the bout, gathering more momentum as the rounds rumbled on. At the end of an exhausting twenty rounds, Harry Wells raised a hand. Leslie took the decision. "The whole twenty rounds were fought with tremendous vigour, and the verdict was, amid great cheering, accorded to the Rhondda man."

The following month at The Tivoli Theatre, Pentre, an Assault-at-Arms was held under the support of a local syndicate connected with the Pentre Athletic Club. It was a Thursday evening on

The Ice Punch

18th August 1910, Bowen was headlining and his opponent was local favourite Jack Titt (Pentre), ex-army and navy lightweight champion. Some of the undercard bouts were also attracting a great amount of interest, in particular between the scientific J. Southway and the dangerous T. Evans, both of Pentre. Evans was known for his brutal punching power but he was unable to land a telling blow and the fight went the distance with Southway said to be displaying a

Dai in fighting pose

remarkable level of intelligence, and ultimately taking the decision. An amusing fight was next when Willie Davies met Johnnie P. Rogers, both Pentre fighters. Onlookers were left amazed and excited by the panto antics of Willie, while also stating that he did show some fine boxing moments. The main event was next and Dai and Jack would fight for £25 a-side and a purse, with Mr B. Meadows being appointed referee although it had previously been reported Mr Giles was to referee, with the Evening Express publicly announcing this was a mistake. Bowen's corner included Dai Stephens, Griff Davies and Lewis Roderick, while in Titt's corner was Jim Southway, Curtis D. Aubrey and another unnamed. Both contestants chose to ask Mr Dan Armstrong, Tonypandy, to assume the office of timekeeper after it had been put to the audience for discussion with no decision forthcoming. Mr Armstrong consented, and then introduced Mr "Brummy" Meadows of the Sporting Life to the ring, while all the time smiling, he bowed in acknowledgement. Mr Meadows then announced he had weighed both Bowen and Titt at ringside, and their respective weights were: Bowen, 9st 2lbs; Titt, 9st 3lbs. Reports of this event were sparse at first, with the announcement the following day that a fine contest had been seen at Pentre, with Bowen dishing out and taking a good deal of punishment while maintaining a good pace as Titt attempted to slow him down. Nine days after the event, the full fight details were published.

"In the first round Titt went straight away for his opponent, but failed to find, Bowen invariably warding off nasty swings and sending lefts and rights home simultaneously. This was repeated up to the fourth round, when Bowen tapped his opponent's claret. Titt did not lose courage and seemed to get the best of the argument in the fifth round. Exchanges characterised the sixth and seventh rounds, although Bowen was the recipient of severe upper cuts which seemed ineffectual. In the ninth Titt found with the left, and following up, brought round a hammer swing which caught Dai on the shoulder. Towards the tenth and eleventh rounds Bowen was aiming at Titt's face, especially the left eye, which appeared bruised. Here Dai was also the recipient of a telling right on the face, but there was no sign of blood following. In the twelfth round Dai found his opponent many times just below the armpits. In the next round Bowen was putting in some telling rights, and Titt found with the right in Bowen's face, which made him retreat towards the ropes, where he marvellously escaped a knock-out, which Titt was trying to confer. In the fourteenth round, Bowen seemed more excellent in spirit, and found his opponent below the left eye, which was now bleeding. In the fifteenth round Titt sent an upper cut, and repeated this just as Bowen was avoiding danger and at the same time finding his opponent in the face, after which they closed and in-fought much. The sixteenth round was in favour of Titt, and in the next Bowen was finding splendidly with the left, and Titt seemed to lean on his opponent. Recovering, Titt again had the best of the eighteenth round, and in the nineteenth Dai safeguarded himself all through and was merely boxing. The twentieth round was decidedly in favour of Bowen, who was conferring lefts and rights very smartly. Cheers were sent up for both at the close, and

FINE CONTEST AT PENTRE.

A fine contest was seen at Pentre on Thursday, when Dai Bowen (Treherbert), a lad of twenty, who holds an unbeaten record in the valleys, fought a twenty-round draw with Jack Titt, ex-Army and Navy light-weight champion, for £25 aside. The local lad administered a good deal of punishment, and took his share in kidney punches, but he continued to box in lively fashion, despite his opponent's wearing-out tactics.

Dai giving as good as he got over twenty rounds

especially for Bowen, who, it was anticipated, would not have gone the whole way. Mr Meadows, in declaring the result, said, as he said before the match, he had come there to see a fair fight and see the winner win. As it happened, he had been unable to separate the men, and a popular verdict-a draw-was given."

As 1910 was drawing to a close, Leslie Williams was getting ready for another battle with Munro Grainger, advertised as a contest for the Bantamweight Championship of Wales. Williams had earned his shot at a title and the fight was creating a huge buzz in the Rhondda as this time around Grainger had been spending time in the camp of Freddie Welsh, sparring hard with the "Welsh Wizard," vastly improving his ring IQ and cleverness. They were to meet at the Millfield A,C, Pontypridd on the 31st October for £50 a-side and a £50 purse. Tickets were on sale for 1s, 2s and 3s, with anyone looking for reserved seats at 5s to contact either the Millfield Athletic Club direct or Mr Harry Marks of Coldstream Terrace, Cardiff. The stakeholders were Mirror of Life and they would be in charge of appointing Mr Bradley as referee, who would soon find himself at the centre of controversy. The doors opened to the general public at 7:30pm and the main event was due around 9pm.

Weigh-in was set for 2pm the same day at the offices of the Evening Express and the lads were to come in at 8st 7lb using scales supplied by W and T Avery, The Hayes, Cardiff. There was a slight delay with it being resolved to give or take 2lbs which both fighters met. Freddie Welsh and Jim Driscoll were present and greeted each other affably with Driscoll favouring the chances of Williams. The prior bouts included "Young" Jenkins of Cilfynydd against Jack Lake of Cardiff as well as a tournament between fighters weighing 7st 6lb, with the winner taking home a gold medal and the runner up a silver medal.

Leslie and Munro were ready and made their way to the ring. With round one underway, Williams was on top of Grainger landing vicious body blows and as the gong went was said to be "simply pummeling his opponent." Grainger fared better in the second round with both having their moments, but as they came out for the third once again Williams took control, severely punishing Grainger to the body and face, and at this point in the fight appearing the only likely winner. They continued to battle furiously in the fourth round as Williams again got the better of the exchanges. Round five started as the fourth had ended with Williams being the aggressor, when suddenly in the middle of the round, he caught Grainger with a devastating body blow that referee Bradley felt was below the waist line, immediately stopping the fight and disqualifying Williams, without so much as a warning. Williams had a huge following and had brought many of his hometown fans with him and they were making their feelings crystal clear, so much so that Mr Bradley was unable to publicly announce his decision. Grainger, to his credit and feeling less than impressed himself due to the uneasiness over the result, offered Williams a re-match on the same terms.

BOXING.

GRAINGER'S WINNINGS IN THE PONTYPRIDD MATCH.

It is understood that the stakes have been paid over to Munro Grainger for his win over Leslie Williams in the bantam-weight championship of Wales at Pontypridd on Monday, and, as there was considerable dissatisfaction over the result of the fight, Grainger is prepared to meet Williams again at 8st. 7lb., weigh in at two o'clock.

Leslie's match with Grainger ended in controversy

There is no doubt Williams would have jumped at this chance, and would have been favoured to reverse the result emphatically. Williams would soon meet Mr Bradley again, but this time it would be in court.

Meanwhile Dai Bowen was sending out challenges, even looking for a re-match of his own with Jack Titt, offering "the best purse in Wales" to fight him over twenty, three minute rounds for £50 a-side and weighing in at 9st 4lb ringside. Awaiting a reply through the Evening Express, another fighter had his sights on such a bout and the prestige attached. J.J Culverhouse sent a reply offering to box Bowen over fifteen or twenty rounds for a sum of £5 but open to £15, and the best purse in Wales. Bowen, less than impressed, returned the favour through the Evening Express offering to fight Culverhouse "over any number of rounds for as much backing as he can find, providing a suitable purse is offered." It went quiet, Culverhouse not being on the same level as Bowen, both in talent and in fame. Then, on the 7th November 1910, the following article appeared, "Seeing that Dai Bowen (Treherbert) is in want of a match, Leslie Williams (Tonypandy) will box him for £25 a-side or any part. A Reply through the Evening Express will lead to

BOXING

Challenge to Dai Bowen

Seeing that Dai Bowen (Treherbert) is in want of a match Leslie Williams (Tonypandy) will box him for £25 aside or any part. A reply through the Evening Express will lead to business.

Leslie's offer to get in the ring with Dai

business." Continuing to impress and show their attitude towards fighting, Bowen and Williams were ready to fight anyone, including each other. Shortly after this, Williams was challenged by Young Walters and he promptly accepted, as was his character, providing a deposit by Walters was paid which would then be covered at once. For now, Bowen and Williams would go on different paths, until a telegram from America changed everything.

Pittsburgh, Pennsylvania was known for its steel mills, smoke filled skies, and hard fighters. Frank Torreyson, a Braddock resident, had a hand in all things sport from baseball to horse racing, and was also a huge booster of the boxing scene. It was said of Torreyson that he "seldom missed a boxing bout in this section and followed the sport from coast to coast." Always lending a hand financially, he would buy upward of half a dozen to a dozen tickets for every fight and if he couldn't attend, he would give them to friends. He also ran a boxing gym that was free to any fighter who wanted to train there. Torreyson knew sports had been good to him, and he believed in sharing the wealth and giving back to the community. This interest led him to take hold of several boxers and bring them out, including sending a message abroad, to Wales, to seek out a couple of talented young boxers who he could manage and develop. His request was answered by Welsh correspondent Charles A. Barnett in the weekly publication known simply as "Boxing."

"Wanted - a smart boxer" was the headline in the January 21st 1911 edition. "A well known American sports promoter has just written to me from across the Atlantic to ask me to recommend a smart boxer for a trip across the water, and the terms, which I do not care to make public, will gladden the heart of the selected man. At present I have two lightweights in view, both good men, but I am in no great hurry to make the selection, as circumstances allow me ample time to do so." Boxing was gathering much needed momentum and two weeks later on Feb 4th, Barnett wrote that a crowd of thousands turned out to see Freddie Welsh box four rounds with the man Leslie Williams had unfinished business

News from South Wales

Wanted—a Smart Boxer.

A well-known American sports promoter has written to me from across the Atlantic to ask me to recommend a smart boxer for a trip over the water, and the terms, which I do not care to make public, will gladden the heart of the selected man. At present I have two lads in view, both good men, but I am in great hurry to make the selection, as circumstances allow me ample time to do so.

"Boxing" - Barnett receiving the request from Torreyson

with, Munro Grainger, at a boxing carnival in Maesteg. Barnett also spoke of an upcoming bout between Williams and another fighter being labelled a "Welsh Wizard" in Pontypool's Young Walters. Sadly, it was not all good news in this week's print and the aforementioned momentum was about to stall.

A week prior, on Saturday Jan 28th, as a dozen excited spectators gathered in an old shoeing shed in the yard of Mr David Allen, a blacksmith from Treherbert, two young lads were stripped down to their waists and lacing up their gloves. Thomas Edmunds who was to referee, had been notified around 1pm of the contest with the desired start time of 3.30pm. Edmunds made his way there, inspected the gloves and softened them well before use. Everyone was in good spirits, including the two boxers, Rees Winchcombe, a colliers assistant from Halifax Terrace and Samuel Morgan, a collier from Tynewydd. The two boys were friends and had arranged this match a fortnight before Christmas for 35 shillings a-side. Winchcombe was said to be laughing from start to finish.

They were to box ten two-minute rounds with one minute intervals. Alexander Allen acted as timekeeper. As the sixth round came to an end, both boxers were looking strong and headed back to their corners. With round seven underway, Morgan got in a blow to Winchcombe's jaw and he fell with a thud, striking his head on one of the old railway sleepers that formed the floor. As he rose, he staggered back and fell hard again. John Henry Winchcombe, brother of Rees, ran towards him and with the help of another young lad picked him up. No one heard his last breath. A doctor was immediately called and the police notified, detaining Morgan and the others at the police station, releasing them once all their statements were gathered. The inquest also took place at Treherbert police station on Monday afternoon and was conducted by Mr R J Rhys, the coroner.

John Winchcombe said he was present at the shoeing shed as the bout commenced around 3:30pm on Saturday. He had heard of the contest taking place a week or two previously but only found out on the afternoon of the fight that it was for a stake. He was there watching the timekeeper as well as for his brother and he believed both boys were evenly matched. The gloves were produced and he believed these were the gloves used in the fight. He knew of no ill feeling between them. When questioned by the foreman of the jury, Mr W Glass, as the last blow landed in the middle of the seventh round he could not tell if his brother fell to the floor on his head. The floor was uneven and the sleepers were rather worn, making it plausible that Rees had slipped.

Referee Thomas Edmunds, after reinforcing the gloves produced were the gloves worn, said he felt Rees Winchcombe had shown no signs of weakness. Morgan had sent a wild swing, a kind of hook, to the left jaw of Winchcombe. It wasn't an overly hard blow and Winchcombe looked dazed but managed to get back to his heels before falling backwards, striking his head with violence. He lay unconscious but was not bleeding. He agreed that the contest had been a friendly one. The timekeeper Alexander Allen said both boys had asked for the use of the shoeing forge on the Friday, the day before the bout. He confirmed he was not given any payment for the use of the shed. Allen also stated "there was an entire absence of roughness and brutality." Edward Doughty of St Albans Terrace, Tynewydd, knew about the bout when it was first arranged and both boys had been trained properly. On Christmas eve Morgan and Winchcombe had put up some of the stake and the remainder had been paid up to date since. He knew both boys well and could also say the contest was fought in a friendly spirit.

Arthur Winchcombe, 17 Blaenycwm Terrace and the father of Rees, said his son would have turned 18 in April, lived with his brother John, and was simply "very fond of boxing." Samuel Morgan, 18 years old with whom Winchcombe boxed, confirmed the contest was arranged a fortnight before Christmas for 35s a-side. He believed he was the slightly heavier of the two. He said Winchcombe came to his feet for a second or two after the right hook and then fell to the floor. He did not put in another blow. Dr W D Henderson attributed the cause of death to concussion and laceration of the brain. Winchcombe had a bruise on his left ear and a superficial abrasion on the inside of his lower lip. There was nothing to suggest a fracture. The pupils of his eyes were evenly dilated. He was of moderate build and Dr Henderson said it was probable that a blood vessel might have given way owing to the fall, but not directly from the blow.

Mr R J Rhys then addressed the jury, "In this case you have to take an unprejudiced view of things. Some people are somewhat opposed to boxing, and go so far as to object to all kinds of sport. It is permitted in this country, and supported by people of importance. Boxing takes place in every part of the kingdom. The question to be considered, was the boxing carried on fairly and was the proper material or gloves used, so that, even if a man received a somewhat hard blow, he would not be hurt severely?" He was aware of other incidents where fighters were incited again and again to box when they were in no fit condition to do so. In this case the two boys were friends and no ill feeling existed between them. They had arranged this contest for the object of testing in a quite friendly spirit the superiority of one or the other. At the opening of the seventh round both boys were as good as the other. It was legal to fight with gloves although he would strongly protest against boxing in such a place as described, and which he had himself seen. The floor should be level and there should be a certain amount of protection. But, still, the contestants chose to go there of their own free will. "You may disapprove of what they did, but they were quite within their rights." A verdict of "Death through misadventure" was returned. The coroner said the verdict was a very proper one.

Barnett had heard rumblings of a tragedy although had little information when he penned the following in his 4th Feb column, "Fatal boxing bout - as I conclude my notes news reaches me of a sad occurrence at a gymnasium in Treherbert, Rhondda. Two young fellows, Samuel Morgan and Hopkin Winchcombe, were having a friendly spar, as I understand it, and Winchcombe was taken ill and died, whether from natural causes or a blow is as yet not clear. I will give further details next week." The death report list of Jan, Feb and Mar 1911 show Rees H Winchcombe, 17 years old, with Hopkin being the young kids middle name that Barnett had been using.

(Continued from page 362.)

£30, and another interesting contest to be shortly brought off is between Young Walters (Pontypool), described by "BOXING" as "a Welsh wizard," and Leslie Williams (Tonypandy), who fought Munro Grainger a while ago.

Fatal Boxing Bout.

As I am concluding my notes news reaches me of a sad occurrence at a gymnasium in Treherbert, Rhondda. Two young fellows, Samuel Morgan and Hopkin Winchcombe, were having a friendly spar, as I understand it, and Winchcombe was taken ill and died, whether from natural causes or a blow is as yet not clear. I will give fuller details next week.

TIRPHIL.

Williams v Young Walters and news of Winchcombe in "Boxing"

CHAPTER 3: The Calling

Bowen and Williams tried their best to continue to fight. Leslie Williams took care of Young Walters over twenty rounds on Monday the 13th Feb at the Millfield A.C. His attention then turned back to Munro Grainger and the controversial decision by referee Mr Frank Bradley to stop the fight on a disqualification. On Monday the 6th March in the City of London Court, Williams was there in person arguing for the value of the agreement made prior to the Grainger fight. Both boys had deposited £25 with Bradley as a stakeholder, and in the turmoil which took place after the decision against Williams, the £25 was never returned, and was now being sought after. Defending Mr Bradley was a Mr Baker, who said Williams lost the contest quite properly, and went on to say the bout took place under an agreement in which Mr Bradley's decision was to be final and that no appeal should be made to the law. In the other corner, defending Williams was a Mr W. S. M. Knight who put forward a much stronger argument. He urged Judge Rentoul that the agreement was void under The Gaming Act as there never was a definite decision as to what was a wagering contract and what was not and this was the state of the law. Although Judge Rentoul said that "an event which depended on a chance was a wagering contract," he did render the agreement null and void after Mr Knight argued that Grainger had been paid improperly. Awarding the amount claimed of £25 plus costs, Williams could now put this behind him and continue making a name for himself as a fighter.

However, the sad loss of Rees Winchcombe was still being talked about. It had a profound effect on the local community and the secretary of the Mid-Rhondda Free Church Council issued a letter asking for boxing contests at the Old Hippodrome, Tonypandy be limited, or stopped altogether. Councillor J.D Williams, who had an interest in the Old Hippodrome, was unaware that such bouts had ever taken place at the building. It now had his full attention, and at a meeting of the Rhondda District Council on Friday 17th March, Councillor Williams gave his assurance that, in compliance with the wishes of the Mid-Rhondda Free Church Council, the practice of boxing bouts at the Old Hippodrome would be stopped. This was met with rapturous applause. Boxing bouts were now becoming increasingly difficult to match and the reporting of fights was almost obsolete. Further concerns were being raised by Rev F. B. Meyer, who stated, "it is useless to call a contest anything but a brutal exhibition, which is no credit to the twentieth century." Bowen and Williams continued as often as was permitted, and their efforts were not going unnoticed.

Charles A. Barnett was as active as anyone behind the scenes, maintaining regular contact with Pittsburgh's Frank Torreyson while also keeping a close eye on how both boxers were performing. Torreyson had sent £20 for Barnett to select a fighter and pay for his travel to America to box under a contract initially lasting one year. Barnett was inevitably swamped with applications from thirsty fighters, but he was a patient man and wanted to get it right. Due to prior engagements, some of the fighters that were being mentioned were unable to make the journey and Barnett chose to hold off, giving it several months as the American fight season was coming to a close. Later in the year Barnett once again received a message from Torreyson, this time asking for two boxers to be sent over. Torreyson sent another £40, eager to make things happen. Barnett was still receiving applications when, some weeks later, he finally announced who would be sailing across the Atlantic. "I have pleasure in announcing that I have selected Leslie Williams (Tonypandy) and Dai Bowen (Treherbert) for the trip to America, and they board the 'Lusitania' this Saturday on a year's tour under the management of Mr Frank W Torreyson of Braddock, Pa., a well known racehorse owner and matchmaker. This gentleman has a finger in nearly every boxing concern of that district, and he is able to run shows throughout the summer, so Leslie and Dai ought to do well."

The contracts were drawn up and proved satisfactory to all when Williams approached Barnett to say he had ordered tailored made suits for the trip. It was important that the lads made a solid impression on their arrival so when they didn't turn up on time, and knowing similar suits would be too costly in America, Barnett once again displayed great patience, telling Williams, "Very well, we will go to the shipping agent and see what other boats are going and I will send another cable to say you will not be going by the 'Lusitania'." Williams was said to be "simply delighted" when he found the world's largest liner was to make her maiden voyage. Barnett immediately booked Williams and Bowen on the *Titanic*.

Bowen's last engagement before getting ready to leave was on Sat 17th Feb 1912 at The Drill Hall in Pentre, where a successful Assault-at-Arms was held in aid of the Gelli locked-out men who had been idle since November 1910. This was the second event to help raise money for the coal workers who had downed tools, a similar meeting being held several months prior and raising £58 which was handed over to the works committee. Bowen would once again be in good company with Jim Driscoll being introduced to the audience by Mr H Davies (The Market), to a hearty reception. Davies announced that "Peerless" Jim was "always ready to lend a helping hand in charitable causes when his engagements permitted." Another notable name participating in the exhibition bouts was a young Jimmy Wilde, known as the "Tylorstown Terror," and who would go on to become one of the world's finest boxers. Jack Titt, a previous opponent of Dai was also part of the programme. The evening ended with Driscoll in a four round bout against Joe Johns. Mr C W Hartnoll of Swansea acted as MC and welcomed both fighters to the ring with Mr J Dowry of Pontypridd being chosen as timekeeper. The fight was said to be "greatly enjoyed" by all those present and as Driscoll left the ring and headed to his dressing room, he was accompanied by music from The Cory Workmen's Prize Band.

There was a tremendous turnout as Treherbert Sports held a smoker in the local Constitutional Club where Bowen was presented with an elegant looking travelling bag as a gift, and they were sent on their way to great acclaim with a promise to Barnett that they would make good use of the gym onboard. Together, they headed to Tenby, jumped

JUST AFTER TITANIC'S LAUNCH.

THE TITANIC BEING TOWED INTO MIDSTREAM AFTER LAUNCH AT BELFAST, IRE.

Titanic appearing in The Boston Globe, Tuesday April 16th 1912

on a train using a warrant issued to Dai, and took the long trip to Southampton.

Around this time, April 2nd and 3rd 1912, the *Titanic* was finished by Harland & Wolff at Belfast harbour and had successfully completed speed trials over a measured mile at the Belfast Lough. The compasses were adjusted, and with the reported "excellent results," headed to Southampton from which port she would sail on April 10th. Eerily, "Steamers to sail from New York" headlined The Baltimore Sun on Monday April 8th, listing all the names of the ships with their intended destinations once they had arrived in America. The *Titanic* was shown sailing back to Southampton on April 20th, in between the steamer Lapland which was headed for Antwerp and the Mesabia headed for London.

The anticipation was building and the passenger rolls were being rapidly filled with many prominent persons from both sides of the Atlantic. The comfort of the *Titanic* was also becoming more apparent with the press covering many of its luxuries. "The *Titanic* posses some interesting innovations. So popular has the Louis XVI restaurant proved on her sister ship Olympic that in the case of the *Titanic* this apartment has been enlarged, and adjacent is a special reception room for the use of passengers taking meals in the restaurant. There are also special suites consisting of bedrooms, sitting rooms, a bathroom and a servants room, each suite possessing its own private deck promenade shut off from the rest of the ship and not overlooked by other passengers." A large crowd had gathered to catch a glimpse of the *Titanic* one last time before she departed, and the effervescent atmosphere was about to be given a shake with the hullabaloo at Southampton docks.

    The *Titanic*, now the world's largest steamer afloat, "had an exciting experience as she was proceeding down Southampton Water." Passing the American line steamer New York and the White Star liner Oceanic, which were berthed alongside each other, she sucked the water between herself and the quay to such an extent that the force broke seven of the strong cables with which the New York was moored. The stern of the New York began drifting helplessly into the path of the oncoming *Titanic*, and but for the quick thinking of the tugs, a collision looked imminent. An eyewitness said, "The crowd watching from the quay was breathless with excitement. The people climbed into railway trucks to see what was going on. As soon as the New York broke loose the *Titanic* reversed her engines and in a brief space of time stopped dead and began to back. Then the tugs Neptune and Vulcan raced at the New York, caught her with ropes by the bow and stern, and tried to lug her back to her place. It was difficult to tell the distances, looking broadside on, but there was not much room to spare between the New York's stern and the *Titanics* side." Had the collision happened, it would likely have resulted in the cancellation of the *Titanic's* maiden voyage.

    The confusion of what happened was evident from first class passengers to those in steerage, Bowen and Williams included. It was, in fact, the perfect send off. They had landed the contracts to fight in America, were sailing on the celebrated *Titanic*, and she was continuing to make headlines before leaving England. As the *Titanic* resumed her voyage, "the throngs on shore gave three rousing cheers." For Captain Edward Smith, and many passengers however, there would be a sense of foreboding in the sea air. The previous September, he had captained her sister ship the Olympic and suffered his first accident in forty years when she was rammed by the British cruiser the Hawke. With severe damage to her hull, Smith turned the Olympic around and headed back to

Southampton. The Olympic, and Captain Smith, were found to be at fault.

Cherbourg, France was the first port of call. Bowen and Williams were creating friendships, were relaxed, and being away from their homes and families, this was as important as training. Mentally, they were right, and with Torreyson travelling to New York to meet them, it would not take long to get them physically ready. Before leaving Southampton they had given Barnett their word that they would use the gym onboard to continue to train, but this would prove to be an ambitious promise. The second class passengers had the opportunity to tour and access some first class spaces at certain times, but this wasn't the case for those sailing on third class tickets. They had access to the forward, poop and aft well deck's which were open air so were able to exercise, however any sparring would have drawn attention. Another problem was immigration laws of the day also meant the separation of steerage class from the rest of the passengers. For now, Bowen and Williams would make use of what they had, and Bowen took the time to write to his mother before they sailed to Queenstown, Ireland.

Dated April 11th 1912, "My dear mother, I am just writing you a few lines before I go sick for I have been very good so far. This is a lovely boat, she is very near so big as Treherbert, she is like a floating palace, against you walk from one end of her to the other you are tired. We are landing in France the time I am writing you this, you don't know whether she is moving or not for she goes very steady. Dear mother, I hope that you won't worry yourself about me, I can tell you I am a lot better than I thought I would be, for we gets plenty of fun on board. We met two Swansea boys at the station, so you see that I get plenty of company. There is hundreds of foreigners on her of every nation. The food we get here is very good but not so good as dear old home. We have no boxing gloves with us, they would be no good if we did have some. Remember me to Martha Jane & Jack & Tommy Ostler, tell Morris & Stephen that if I will feel like I do now when I land in Yankee Land I shall be alright. I shan't give you no address now, not until I land for it won't be worth. I did not see David Rees in Southampton at all. Remember me to all I know, tell Stephen to tell all the boys that I am enjoying myself alright so far. If James tell you that I have not wrote to him, tell him that I can't do it very good now, you can show him this if you like, for it will be the same I shall have to say now for the time being as I am telling you. I hope you will excuse the pencil for I have no pen and ink, so cheer up now mother, for I am in the pink, so don't vex. I think I will draw to a close now in wishing you all my best love. From your loving son, David John."

After posting the letter, and including the railway warrant stamped for Tenby Parcels office, they continued on their way with their new found friends. Unnervingly, on April 15th 1912, some newspapers began printing fantastical, if not confusing headlines. "Slowly going toward Halifax" said The Montreal Star as an unofficial dispatch stated that word had been received of an accident late the night before, but that "the *Titanic* was still afloat and was making her way slowly toward Halifax." The families of both lads had their concerns temporarily eased when P. A. S Franklin, vice president of the White Star Line, released the following statement at 9am on the morning of the 15th. "We have absolute confidence in the *Titanic*. We believe the boat is absolutely unsinkable, and although she may have sunk at the head or bow, we know that the boat would remain on the water." Franklin went on to say he had no concerns over the fact that no messages were being received as the *Titanic* must have been in contact with other steamers and sent all the messages she wanted to send. He then said he was deeply sorry for the "annoyance, and inconvenience to our passengers."

Approximately an hour later Franklin authorised a further statement. "No alarm for *Titanic's* passengers" was the bulletin as he also stated "the officials were perfectly satisfied that there was no cause for alarm regarding the safety of the passengers or the ship, as they regard the *Titanic* as being practically unsinkable." This time he strayed from his morning line, instead saying the absence of messages was not serious and most likely due to "atmospheric disturbances or other causes." He ended by again reinforcing the *Titanic* could withstand any exterior damage, and citing the names of other ships that were on their way to help, notably the White Star Line steamers the Olympic and the Baltic as well as The Virginian from the Allan Line. It seemed as though the drama at Southampton docks had been overshadowed by a commotion out at sea, but nothing more than that.

Franklin made a further announcement later that afternoon, stating the Virginian was alongside the *Titanic*, as were the Carpathia and the Parisian steamships. Franklin used this as a means of validating his belief that reports coming in of the *Titanic's* sinking were mistaken, "I do not believe that is possible." Nobody at this stage either considered, or wanted to consider, the chilling events that had unfolded in what would become known as "Iceberg Alley." Families and friends of the passengers were becoming increasingly concerned, and back in Wales, those eager to hear news about Dai and Leslie were growing more disturbed by the wave of bad news coming in. Wireless operators stationed at the Charlestown Navy Yard confirmed they were aware of some communication between the *Titanic* and the Virginian shortly after midnight. However, due to the wireless station based at Wellfleet sending and receiving press material around this time, they were unable to pick up or make sense of any of the *Titanic's* messages.

The station at Cape Race had managed to receive them however, along with the station at St. Johns which had also gathered several, and it soon became clear the *Titanic* had struck an iceberg. "Sinking by the head and women are being rushed into the lifeboats!" were the last words that manifested in the wireless room of the Virginian from the *Titanic*. Franklin was astounded but remained satisfied there was no real danger. The weather was said to be calm and clear, making the transfer of passengers to lifeboats relatively risk free, and he continued to defy anyone that suggested the *Titanic's* water-tight compartments couldn't keep her on the surface. To others, and to those close to Dai and Leslie, it was more distressing. The reports of the *Titanic* sinking at around midnight, that women were being taken off, and that wireless communications were broken half an hour later were viewed with the utmost anxiety. Franklin, growing more perturbed, sent the following wireless message to Captain Smith, the *Titanic's* commander, "Anxiously awaiting information, full particulars, probable disposition of passengers."

Reports of her sinking were gathering pace. Some newspapers focused on the estimated number of deaths while others homed in on her worth and the large amount of valuable cargo onboard. A list of the greatest sea disasters appeared including the General Slocum fire and sinking in 1904 and the SS Utopia tragedy in 1892, when a wireless message from Captain Haddock of the Olympic confirmed everyone's fears, "Horrible disaster - all but 670 lost." As if dragging Wales and the world to its knees with him, Franklin broke down along with several other grey haired veteran seamen from the White Star offices as it was settled, "That the greatest catastrophe in marine history has occurred to a vessel of their line is admitted by the officials of the White Star Steamship company in New York."

Foundering approximately four hours after striking the iceberg, no man was given any hope of survival when it was pointed out any person in close vicinity would have been unable to escape her great suction as she took her final dive to the bottom. The liner Carpathia was noted as the first to arrive, picking up all the *Titanic's* lifeboats in which most persons were women and children, while believing many women and children had also perished. The following message was then described by the steamer Olympic, "Carpathia returning to New York with women and children numbering 866 aboard. Grave fears are entertained for the rest." With Torreyson looking for the fighting lads, and their families back home desperate to hear from them, the following appeared in the Pittsburgh Post-Gazette, "Leslie Williams and Dave Bowen, the Welsh fighters, who were to come to this country and work under the management of Frank Torreyson of McKeesport, were on the *Titanic* which went down near Cape Race. Torreyson is now in New York. He went there to greet them upon their arrival."

Elsewhere, reporters were attempting to remain realistic, if not slightly optimistic. "Husbands separated from their wives, parents from their children, the scenes must have been heart-breaking when the awful fact was realised that the thousands literally faced death. Without the absolute and definite knowledge that all missing are lost, there is a slight hope that some may have been rescued, and some homes may still be happy over the safety of a loved one."

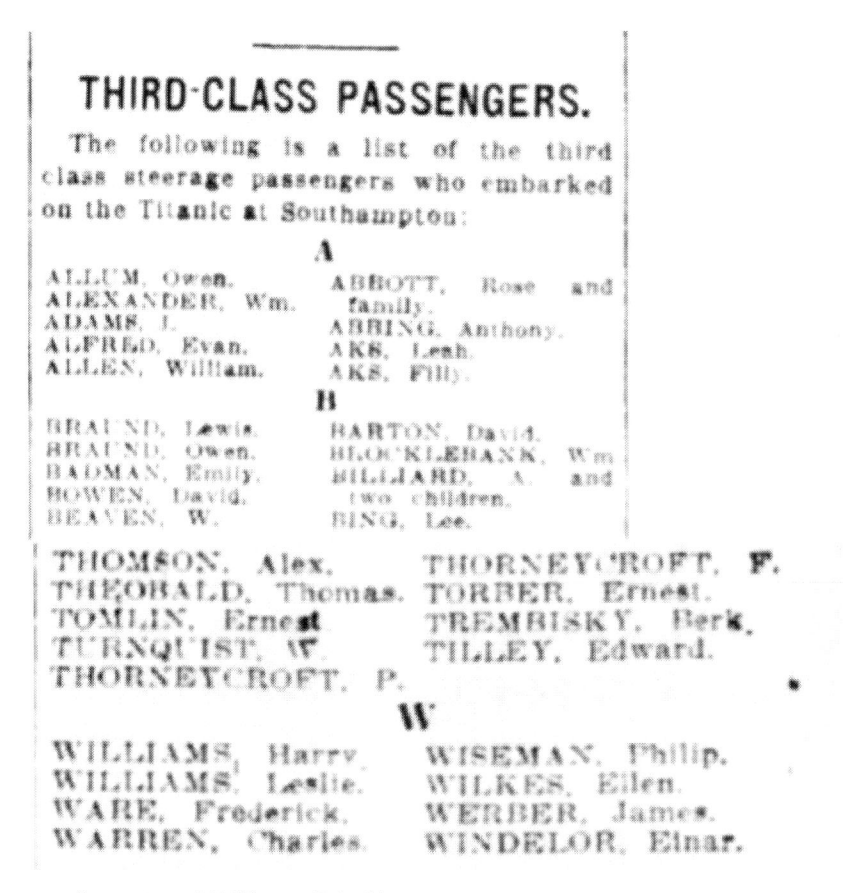

THIRD-CLASS PASSENGERS.

The following is a list of the third class steerage passengers who embarked on the Titanic at Southampton:

A

ALLUM, Owen.
ALEXANDER, Wm.
ADAMS, J.
ALFRED, Evan.
ALLEN, William.

ABBOTT, Rose and family.
ABBING, Anthony.
AKS, Leah.
AKS, Filly.

B

BRAUND, Lewis.
BRAUND, Owen.
BADMAN, Emily.
BOWEN, David.
BEAVEN, W.

BARTON, David.
BLOCKLEBANK, Wm.
BILLIARD, A. and two children.
BING, Lee.

THOMSON, Alex.
THEOBALD, Thomas.
TOMLIN, Ernest.
TURNQUIST, W.
THORNEYCROFT, P.

THORNEYCROFT, F.
TORBER, Ernest.
TREMBISKY, Berk.
TILLEY, Edward.

W

WILLIAMS, Harry.
WILLIAMS, Leslie.
WARE, Frederick.
WARREN, Charles.

WISEMAN, Philip.
WILKES, Ellen.
WERBER, James.
WINDELOR, Einar.

Bowen and Williams listed in steerage

Amongst the confusion, some of the media were listing Bowen and Williams as second class passengers, as well as stating a sister of Bowen was with them and was alive and well on the Carpathia. All of this was quickly discredited when a list of third class passengers on the *Titanic*, as far as it could be compiled, was given out at the offices of the White Star Line. Bowen and Williams were both shown as having embarked the ill-fated vessel at Southampton on third class tickets, while

WHITE STAR LINER TITANIC

Largest Steamship Afloat, Which Collided With an Iceberg Off the Banks of Newfoundland While on Her Initial Trip.

The Titanic pictured in "The Stevens Point Journal"

the female listed with the name Bowen was in fact a New Yorker with no relation to Dai.

"Boxers drowned" and "Pugs probably lost" were just some of the headlines making the news as more and more stories were being received stating the boys from Wales were amongst those who went down with the *Titanic*. The first word back home appeared in The Rhondda Leader when it printed "some passengers from our own locality were among those on board," followed by naming Leslie Williams and Dai Bowen as professional boxers who were mixed up in the calamity at sea. Eyewitness accounts were more haunting. One survivor recalled, as they slipped quietly away in a lifeboat, "Her great bulk outlined in black against the starry sky, every porthole and saloon blazing with light. Then with a quiet, slanting dive she disappeared beneath the waters and our eyes had looked for the last time on the gigantic vessel we had set out on from Southampton last Wednesday. And then there fell on the ear the most appalling noise that human being ever listened to - the cries of hundreds of our fellow beings struggling in the icy cold water crying for help, with a cry that we knew could not be answered." The captain of the Carpathia placed all private messages ahead of press releases and sent

PUGS PROBABLY LOST.

(U. P. Special Service)

New York, April 18.—Dave Bowen and Leslie Williams, two British boxers, are believed to have been among those who went down with the Titanic. They were on their way to this country to make a number of matches.

The aforementioned "Pugs Probably Lost" headline

marconigrams free of charge to anxious relatives, none of which were received in the households of Bowen or Williams.

CHAPTER 4: The Fatal Blow

The Mackay-Bennett cable ship, captained by Frederick H. Lardner, was sent to the scene with the disheartening task of recovering bodies. Officials of the White Star Line were checking some of the names against their passenger lists when they started announcing the identification of some of the dead. Amongst the passengers found, Leslie William's name appeared. For his family in Wales, this was the concrete news they were fearing. Painfully, Dai was not one of those mentioned, his body

TWO WELSH BOXERS DIE ON TITAN

Leslie Williams and David Bowen Bound for Scranton, Persh on Liner.

FORMER'S BODY RECOVERED

Two Welsh pugilists, Leslie Williams and David Bowen, bound for the Pennsylvania coal regions to share in the glory and proceeds of the prize-fights which have been permitted here since the last legislature lifted the prohibition against such contests, died on the Titanic, according to information received here yesterday by Samuel Howells, a local fighter, who himself emigrated to this country from Wales six months ago.

Both Bowen and Williams embarked on the Titanic at Southampton, and their names appear on the passenger lists of third class passengers. The first definite information received by Samuel Howells was in an Associated Press dispatch published in The Tribune-Republican yesterday stating that the body of one Leslie Williams had been recovered by the cable ship Mackay-Bennett at the scene of the Titanic disaster. This, coupled with the fact that both of the fighters were expected on the ship, has convinced the friends of the pugilists that both perished on the liner.

The boys had perished

either being recovered but not identified, or not recovered at all. Both boys did appear in the "Register Of Deceased Passengers," listed as third class passengers and their occupation as boxers. Next to Dai's name, "supposed drowned," was scribbled in black ink. Williams was also named in the "Disposition of Bodies" list showing those recovered by the Mackey-Bennett. The boxing world, upon hearing the news, started to pull together. Not far from Pittsburgh, Sammy Howells, who had emigrated from Wales six months prior and was boxing out of Scranton, Pennsylvania, said that Bowen and Williams were clever fighters and would have been able to "share in the fun of fighting before Scranton crowds." He finished by saying "if they were both on the boat and either had survived there would be no delay about coming to Scranton. They were sturdy boys and I believe now that Williams' body has been found, that both were lost at sea." George McDonald, the manager of Matt Wells who had won the British Lightweight Championship by defeating Freddie Welsh, was to take charge of the arrangements for Leslie's body to be buried in New York and he wrote to the Principal Secretary's Office requesting The White Star Co hold the body of Williams. Wells was fighting Packey McFarland on 26th April in Madison Square Garden and

McDonald had planned to use both Dai and Leslie to help get him in shape, with his trainer Dr. Doolings saying, "Bowen and Williams had been counted on to aid Wells greatly in his work-outs." The Mackay-Bennett would be at sea for around two weeks, and very quickly encountered difficulties in preserving the bodies. Hard decisions were looking imminent.

Back in Wales the boys were being remembered and for the first time their pictures appeared in the press. Bowen was said to be a very popular young lad and was making great strides in the noble art. His fight with Jack Titt was said to be "witnessed by a tremendous crowd at the Tivoli, Pentre. He fought with pluck and perseverance." His passion originated in the local gymnasiums and he later ran his own gymnasium, which was almost entirely dedicated to boxing. Such was the adoration for Dai, numerous letters of condolence were being received by his family, and in particular his mother.

Williams was a very familiar name with the Rhondda people. The locals were aware of his "brilliant career, who was progressing in the boxing world by leaps and bounds." He was a well respected and admired young man by all who crossed paths with him. The boys had such a following that it was described, "Throughout the churches and chapels of the Rhondda, on Sunday last, 21st April, the *Titanic* bandsmen's hymn, 'Nearer my God, to Thee,' was sung with great pathos." Special prayers

DAI BOWEN.   LES. WILLIAMS.

Dai and Leslie appear in the Rhondda Leader

were offered up for the bereaved families, whilst in many cases memorial sermons were preached, followed by renderings of the "Dead March."

The hymn was also being played by bands throughout the district, bringing many to shed a tear. Two days later on Tuesday 23rd April at the County Club in Tonypandy, of which Leslie was a member, a concert was held in the memories of both boys and a vote of condolence was passed with the widow and relatives of Williams and the relatives of Bowen.

The following evening, Wednesday 24th April, a large number of people descended upon the Miskin Hotel, Trealaw, to thrash out arrangements for a scheme to benefit the expectant widow and child of Leslie and the mother of Dai. Elected to chair was Mr W. P. Clark of Tonypandy with Mr J. Afan Jenkins chosen as secretary. Before the meeting began, there was a moment's silence for the bereaved families. The first idea brought to the table was the suggestion of a gymkhana and military sports event to be held on the Mid-Rhondda Athletic Grounds in Tonypandy. Initially this was thrown out by Jenkins, but after further discussion, and considering the Athletic Grounds had been offered gratuitously by the Committee of the Social and Athletic Club for that sole purpose, it was decided that this was exactly the right thing to do. Those present then passed a vote of thanks to the committee.

Furthermore, they had a contingency in place incase of wet weather. Mr Dudley Harcourt, manager of the Empire, Tonypandy, had given his authority that on the day, should the weather be against them, his building would be at their disposal and he had left Mr Dan Armstrong, Tonypandy, in charge if this materialised. This news brought with it a hearty round of applause. With this agreed, the next step was to form district committee's and these would cover areas such as Cardiff and also the Merthyr and Aberdare areas. A vote of thanks was then passed to the Rhondda Leader and Messrs Evans and Short, as both had offered to provide free of charge memoriam cards of the two boys. These keepsakes would then be retailed for a small sum with the entire proceeds going to the fund. It was then decided to hold a further meeting at the Miskin Hotel on Friday evening, April 26th at 8 o'clock, to discuss the finer details. Mr Albert Griffiths of Miskin was elected as treasurer. Before concluding, it was announced The Porth tramway men had arranged a church parade and memorial service for Sunday 5th May, with the collections en route and those earned in the chapel be given directly to this relief fund. The Tramway Silver band were also being sought after to perform by the tramway mens delegate. Others had promised to assist,

Gus Venn of the London Volunteering offered his assistance, and "Peerless" Jim Driscoll, as always, was willing.

While things in Wales were moving forward, more disheartening news was coming out of the disaster. The Mackay-Bennett had docked in Halifax on April 30th and Captain Lardner, weather beaten and sounding crushed, announced that his vessel was unable to bring back all the bodies recovered, some of which had been identified. When asked why some bodies were buried at sea, Lardner shook his head and gave the following explanation. "When we left Halifax we took on board all of the embalming fluid in the city. That was only enough to care for seventy bodies. It wasn't expected that we would find bodies in such great quantities. The undertaker didn't think these bodies would keep more than three days at sea, and as we expected to be out more than two weeks, we had to bury them. They received the full service for the dead before they slid over the rail." The body of a young man was given the number fourteen, and the contents of his pockets and valuables were placed in a canvas bag and given the same number. This method of numbering the bodies with the canvas bags enabled some identifications to be made.

When bag fourteen was searched, it was confirmed that the young man committed to the deep was Leslie Williams.

He was dressed in a green overcoat, blue serge suit, a red striped shirt and two scarves. His belongings were recorded as two pocket books, two gold rings, one pair of silver cuff links, ticket, papers, knife etc. He also had £3 10s and $30 in gold, with £2 6s 6d in silver and odd coppers. For Leslie's wife back home this would cause some concern. She had heard and read this was his recovered belongings, but on receipt, she was presented with less than this amount. Managing the belongings was down to Frederick F. Mathers, the Deputy Provincial Secretary of the Halifax office and after some correspondence with The White Star Line, it was agreed the lesser amount was correct, this being $15 in gold and not $30 as originally thought, and lesser coin. It was concluded that they found it "remarkable that the inventories were, in view of the circumstances, as accurate as they proved to be." Leslie was also noted as travelling on a 3rd class ticket and living at 59 Primrose St, Tonypandy. Canon Kenneth C, Hinds, assistant rector of the All Saints Cathedral in Halifax, read the service for Leslie. He would be one of fifty-seven identified bodies listed by the White Star offices as buried at sea from the Mackey-Bennett. His body was said to be badly mutilated, and many others were bruised and broken. When questioned, Lardner said they must have been carried against spars, against stanchions and other parts of the vessel when the water rushed them as it swept her decks.

In some quarters, the tragedy was said to have been foretold. Morgan Robertson wrote "Wreck of the Titan," previously known as "Futility" in 1898, fourteen years before the *Titanic* disaster. As with the *Titanic*, the Titan was said to be unsinkable, was the largest ship afloat and did not carry enough lifeboats for all her passengers. The Titan struck an iceberg near midnight in April, in the North Atlantic. Robertson was said to have felt this kind of catastrophe in the icy Atlantic waters was

Morgan Robertson

always a possibility and attributed this to his deep maritime knowledge, others felt that due to the similarities with the real life events, he must have had clairvoyant like abilities.

Back home a further meeting took place at the Miskin Hotel on Friday evening, May 3rd, chaired again by Mr W. P. Clark. Here, the date was set for the gymkhana and Assault-at-Arms to be held on Thursday June 20th, on the Mid-Rhondda Athletic Grounds. A committee was then formed comprising five delegates from Treherbert, five from Mid-Rhondda, one from Treorchy, one from Pentre, three from Porth (including a tramway mens delegate), two from Ferndale, two from Aberdare, two from Merthyr, two from Cardiff and two from Pontypridd. At the earlier meeting of April 24th, the discussed parade at Porth went ahead on Sunday night, headed by the Tramways Silver Band. Collections were made on behalf of the families of Leslie and Dai as the procession weaved through the principal streets of Porth, finishing at the English Congregational Chapel where Rev. R. E. Salmon gave a sermon on "The power of music." Throughout the evening, "Nearer my God to Thee" and the "Dead March" echoed around the walls as the band played continuously, while Mr Wm. Davies spoke of "The Sailor's Grave."

Everyone that could be there was in attendance and the service was said to be a great success.

Charitable events were happening all over the world as the tragedy had affected so many households. Boxing promoter and manager Frank Cancilla proposed a series of bouts be held at the Empress theatre in Winnipeg on Friday May 10th. The Winnipeg Boxing Club was in full support and offered the following fighters for Cancilla to select from, "Chuck" Scully, "Young" Mulhall, Billie Brown, "Big" Mack and Joe Thorburn. Another fighter from the club, "Young" O'Brien was unable to participate owing to injuries to both hands, and was said to be very apologetic. The boys were ready to meet any fighter of the same weight in the city for charity. Other fighters started throwing their names in, with Ernie Sundberg offering to meet anyone at 125lbs and the clever little Italian lightweight Charlie Lucca confirmed. The Rhondda Leader told of a further programme in Porth, this time at the Palace on Friday, May 10th and raising £9 5s for the *Titanic* Relief Fund. The night included pictures relative to the disaster, performances by the Cymmer Club Harmonic Society and a recitation of "The Wreck of the Stella" by Mr Garfield Thomas. Gifts were presented, including what was described as "a very unique item" submitted by a singer and dancer from Ferndale. The Mid-Rhondda Athletic Grounds proved again their doors were always open and was the venue booked for a charity football match to be held on Saturday May 11th between Mid-Rhondda and St. Cynon's (Rhondda Valley League Champions). Every penny raised would be evenly split and handed to the widow of Leslie Williams and the mother of Dai Bowen.

As the date of the gymkhana and Assault-at-Arms drew closer further meetings were held, this time at the Miskin hotel as well as the nearby Bute hotel. Mr Afan Jenkins submitted a lengthy report outlining the final arrangements which was then passed to the executive committee to mull over. In the Miskin on Wednesday May 15th, the executives sat around a table where it was decided that the report be accepted as read. Approved and ready to go, the final meeting between the committee, supporters and friends of the relief fund took place at the Greyhound Hotel in Pontypridd on Wednesday May 22nd, commencing at 7:30pm, ending in a round of applause as the realisation set in that the lives of Dai and Leslie would be celebrated in the grandest fashion.

Near the end of May, Mr Jenkins contacted the "Daily Mail," requesting the visit of one of their aeroplanes to the grounds on the day of the gymkhana and Assault-at-Arms. Jenkins received a reply. "Dear Sir, in reply to your communication dated the 31st May, I am afraid that it will not be possible for the Daily Mail aeroplane to visit the Rhondda on the date stated, June 20th, as demonstrations have been promised in Plymouth, throughout Cornwall, Gloucester etc...If it is possible to arrange a flight to your fete, this will be done, and you will be notified.

TITANIC DISASTER.
In Memoriam.

MID-RHONDDA
Athletic Grounds
TONYPANDY.

Gymkhana and Assault-at-Arms

On the above Grounds,

Next Thursday, June 20th.

President—L. W. LLEWELYN, Esq., Llwynypia.

UPWARDS OF 200 ARTISTES WILL APPEAR, INCLUDING THE CHAMPION WRESTLERS, BOXERS, AND GYMNASTS.

Grand Mounted Military Tournament.

3 BANDS 3

TUG-OF-WAR COMPETITIONS.

MINSTREL TROUPES AND ALL THE BEST LOCAL TALENT WILL APPEAR.

Gates open at 2 p.m.; Commence at 3.

PROCEEDS IN AID OF BEREAVED FAMILIES OF LES. WILLIAMS (TONYPANDY) AND DAI BOWEN (TREHERBERT).

ADMISSION, 6d.; ENCLOSURE, 1/-; RESERVED SEATS, 2/6.

Ticket for the event in aid of the Bowen and Williams families

Yours faithfully, Valentino Smith, manager, Circulation department."
Not to be disheartened, Jenkins pulled on some powerful people, that being Charles A Barnett, Councillor Tom Evans of the Rhondda District, Councillor Enoch Davies of Treherbert and Mr Wm. Johns, miners agent. Together they travelled to London on Tuesday June 11th June and urged the "Daily Mail" to give the people of Rhondda the opportunity of witnessing a flight by an aeroplane. It was agreed that if possible, this would be done however the plane was already booked for the date and would never make the Rhondda Athletic Grounds. Barnett also wrote in Boxing around this time that twenty thousand tickets had already been sold for the *Titanic* benefit. On the tickets it stated over two hundred artists would perform from boxers, gymnasts and wrestlers, with the admission price set at sixpence, the enclosure selling for one shilling and the reserved seats costing two shillings and sixpence. While in London, Barnett took the opportunity to contact all the star boxers of the day in the hope they would be willing to lend a hand.

The event itself, under the presidency of Mr L. W. Llewelyn and owing to the energy and enthusiasm of the committee, including chairman Mr W. P. Clark, treasurer Mr Albert D. Griffiths and secretary

Mr Afan J. Jenkins, surpassed everyone's expectations. Twenty four thousand eager spectators gathered on the grounds to witness the show. Throughout the day and on different platforms, various artists performed as the boxers and wrestlers engaged. Tenors and baritones sang, bands played on the grass as people gathered and danced, one of them being the Cory Workmen's Band, and comedians were drawing laughter from the audience. Exhibitions including swordsmanship, sectional tent pegging and fencing were given by a host of military personnel while champion wrestlers battled.

Charles Barnett had wanted to pull on as many famous boxers as he could and there was a tremendous turnout of pugilists to aid with the benefit. Barnett had signed up middleweight amateur champion of Wales Harry Davies of Maesteg, the household names of Digger Stanley and Eddie Morgan, Morgan himself was one of those considered by Barnett to head to Pittsburgh, as well as other famous fighters of the day such as Young Walters and Badger O'Brien. As with these charitable events, the crowd were thrilled when "Peerless" Jim Driscoll, featherweight champion of the world and an acquaintance of both Dai and Leslie, wrapped his hands and put on the gloves for his bout. The other big name and crowd pleaser who Barnett had contacted and was happy to appear was the Tylorstown Terror, Jimmy Wilde. Nobody present could have anticipated such a resounding, successful celebration of the lives of the popular Rhondda lads.

A full list of participants emerged and was as follows: the military personnel, Sergt-Major Knowles and Sergt-Major Morrions of the 7th Queen's Own Hussars, Sergt-Major Giddings of the 7th Royal Lancers, Sergt-Major Williams of the Royal Engineers, Sergt Branch and Sergt Williams of the Glamorgan Yeomanry, ex Sergt-Major Webber and Sergt Scratton of the Mounted Police, Cardiff and Corporal Driscoll, Llandaff. The boxers were: Jim Driscoll, feather-weight champion of the world, the renowned Wallie Pickard, Newmarket, Badger O'Brien, Cardiff, "Young" Walters, Pontypool, Arthur Evans, Tirphil, Bat McCarthy, Cardiff, Curley Pullman, Merthyr, "Young" Beynon, Port Talbot, Jack Jones, Aberaman, Lewis Williams, Penygraig, W. Phillips, Penygraig, Dai Matthews, Trealaw F. Davies, Ferndale, Trevor Francis, Jack Harrison, middle-weight champion of England, Digger Stanley, bantam-weight champion of the world, Eddie Morgan, prospective bantam-weight champion of the world, Jimmy Wilde, Tylorstown, prospective fly-weight champion of the world, Harry Davies, Maesteg, middle-weight amateur champion of Wales, Jack Phillips, Aberaman, W. H. Thomas, Cardiff, W. H. McCarthy, Cardiff, E. L. Davies, Porth, Bandy Davies, Pontypridd, Jimmy Rees, Porth, Sam Owen, Aberaman, Kid Evans, Trehafod, "Young" Beddoe, Pontypridd, and the "Young" Midgets, Pentre. Wrestling bouts were given by: Arthur Sax, London, Kid Batten, Taunton, Llew Williams, Pentre, Will Williams, Treorchy, Will Hughes, Pentre, Ned Bevan, Pentre, Harry Morris, Caerau, Dai Jenkins, Caerau, Bert Hooper, Tonypandy and Tom Howells, Llwynypia. The entertainers were: Tenors - W. Todd Jones, Treherbert, Gomer Jones, Treherbert, Ben Thompson, Treherbert, T. Todd Jones, Treherbert, Richard Davies, Treherbert, H. Selby, Treherbert, Owen Treharne, Pentre, Joe Jones, Pentre, William Davies, Porth, Mog Edwards, Mountain Ash, William Williams, Trealaw, J. Morgan, Tonypandy, and J. Lloyd, Tonypandy. Baritones - Sam Price, Treherbert, Dai Davies, Treherbert, Jack Jones, Treherbert, D. J. Thomas, Treorchy, Dai Evans, Treorchy, Tom Davies, Mardy, Rowley Jones, Porth, J. H. Rogers, Tylorstown, Moses Jenkins, Mountain Ash, R. O. Jones, Tonypandy, and Ted Evans, Trealaw. Comedians: Reggie Morgan (the boy comedian),

Troedyrhiw, Ellis Share, Treherbert, Dai Hooper, Treherbert, Will Floyd, Treherbert, Will Evans, Treherbert, Jack Granfield, Treorchy, George Williams, Pentre, Will Hatton, Pentre, Will Woodward, Pentre, and Jack Twissell, Tonypandy. Accompanists: D. M. Hammond, W. J. Jenkins, Trealaw, D. J. Howells, R. Walters, Treorchy, and J. L. Rees, Ferndale.

For the families of both boys, cash payments were to be made once the takings had been counted and verified, and was said to be a considerable amount that "will keep the bailiffs at bay for all time." Strangely, away from the Gymkhana, two tennis players, B. N. Williams and Karl Behr eyeballed each other in the fourth round of the Longwood tennis singles tournament in Boston. Both had been on the *Titanic* and both were picked up by a life raft after some time in the water. Dai and Leslie, at one time, were close to meeting in the ring.

The committee gathered in the Miskin with Mr W. P. Clark in the chair on the evening of Wednesday 3rd July. Anxious to ensure the families of Bowen and Williams received their benefits as soon as possible, it was agreed that all tickets, subscriptions books and cash be returned to treasurer Mr A. D. Griffiths at the Miskin by no later than Monday July 15th. Things didn't move as fast as they had hoped and the committee were forced to meet again in August, deciding that the closing date to collect outstanding monies would be moved to the end of the month, that of the 31st August. R. M. Rees, Checkweigher from Tonypandy and Geo. E Roddy, Superintendent Rhondda Tramway Co, Porth, were appointed as auditors and the balance sheet would be made available so that the distribution of funds could begin. This delay caused the committee to agree on an early payout to the families to assist them while the final measures took place, and the widow of Leslie was forced to come out publicly and state this was the case. "Rhondda *Titanic* Benefit Fund - To the editor of the Rhondda Leader. Sir, A rumour having got circulated in the district to the effect that the committee of the above fund have not advanced me any of the funds. I wish, through the columns of the Rhondda Leader, to state I have received two donations from the officials of the fund, and I am grateful for the interest taken by the committee on my behalf, and for their services in assisting me and my children in the great loss we have sustained. Thanking you for inserting this disclaimer, I remain yours." Mrs Leslie Williams, Primrose Street, Tonypandy, August 24th, 1912.

Chairman..W. P. CLARK, Tonypandy
Vice-Chairman....................................R. SAUNDERS, Treherbert

	£	s.	d.
Subscriptions	57	4	6
Tickets Sold	128	17	9
Received at Gate	95	12	6
Stall Standings	2	18	6
Memorial Cards (per W. D. Jones)	2	15	0
Receipts from Kid Evans' Photo	0	6	0
Sale of Right of Programmes (per " Rhondda Leader ")	10	0	0
Sale of Timber (D. W. Thomas)	9	0	0
Return of Fee (Amateur Gymnastic Association)	0	5	0
	£306	19	3

Income details of the charity event

With all monies and tickets returned, the balance sheet put on the table and a detailed list of every name that had purchased a ticket, the committee got together on Wednesday 11th September and agreed to call a general meeting in the Assembly Room of the Miskin at 8pm on Wednesday evening, 18th September. Everyone involved and interested

	£	s.	d.
Treasurer............A. D. GRIFFITHS, Miskin Hotel, Trealaw			
Secretary.........................J. AFAN JENKINS, Tonypandy			
Printing	35	12	3
Artistes	26	18	3
Billposting	10	15	0
Timber for Staging, &c.	16	5	0
Erecting Stands, &c.	5	10	0
Police Services	2	11	8
Labour and Haulage	3	3	0
Drapings for Stages	2	2	0
Postage, Telegrams and Telephone	7	2	0
Train and Car Fares of Committee	0	13	8
Clerical Assistance	2	10	0
Expenses re "Daily Mail" Interview re Aeroplane	4	4	0
Fancy Dresses for Advertisement	1	5	3
Entrance Fee to Amateur Gymnastic Association	0	5	0
Advances to Dependents	19	0	0
Ironmongery	0	5	7
Balance for Distribution	168	13	7
	£306	19	3
Net Profit	£187	15	7

Overall net gain of £187, 15s and 7d

in the event were invited and the Vicar of Llwynypia, Rev D. W. Davies, kindly agreed to attend and preside over the arrangements for the distribution of the funds.

Here, it was unanimously agreed to appoint Rev Davies and Mr T. P. Jenkins as trustee's in the interest of Mrs Williams, with Mr Sidney Mainwaring and Mr Robert Saunders looking after the interests of Mrs Bowen. A genial vote closed the meeting and Rev Davies was thanked

The Ice Punch

for helping and watching over proceedings. The money raised was divided evenly between the two bereaved families. Although this was no consolation, it was of some comfort to know how well received the boys

	£	s.	d.		£	s.	d.
Wattstown Club	0	7	0	Mr. Arthur Evans, Tirphil	1	11	7
Hibernian Club, Gelli	1	15	0	Mr. I. Cable, Ystrad	0	19	0
Ynyshyl Conservative Club	1	15	6	Ferndale Imperial Club	0	6	6
Mr. Howell Jones, Tylorstown	0	7	0	Mr. T. Clark, Aberdare	1	1	0
Mr. Will Jones, Boilermaker, Tonypandy	5	9	0	Mr. G. Wells, Trealaw	1	2	0
Do. do. do.	2	1	6	Clydach Vale Democratic Club	2	11	0
Do. do. do.	3	8	0	Treorchy Conservative Club	1	0	0
Do. do. do.	3	10	0	Blaenclydach Liberal Club	0	2	6
Labour Club, Clydach Vale	2	9	0	Mr. E. Rees, De Winton Hotel, Tonypandy	0	9	0
Mr. Rees Edwards	1	1	6	Mr. Tom Jones, Lewis Arms	1	12	0
Do. do.	0	7	6	Mr. W. Davies, Black Diamond Hotel	0	5	0
Deri Conservative Club	0	18	6	Mr. I. Tucker, Glamorgan Hotel	0	16	0
Mr. Meadows, Stationmaster, Tonypandy	2	10	0	Labour and Progressive Club, Penygraig	0	2	6
Mr. Ted Morris, Swan Hotel, Penygraig	0	11	6	Mr. Ivens, Turberville Hotel, Penygraig	0	5	0
Mr. E. S. Philpotts	7	0	0	Mr. M. Davies, Royal Hotel, Trealaw	0	17	0
Mr. Tom Jenkins	4	1	0	Mr. A. D. Griffiths, Miskin Hotel, Trealaw	0	15	0
Mr. Jim Wilde, Tylorstown	1	8	6	Mr. Thomas, Welcome Home, Treherbert	1	7	0
Mr. Ted Mayo, Tonypandy	0	16	0	Marxian Club, Blaenclydach	0	2	0
Ynysyfeio Colliery	13	9	0	Mr. S. Barkway, Tonypandy	0	5	0
Gilfach Goch Conservative Club	2	16	8	Mr. J. B. Cording, Athletic Club, Tonypandy	1	17	0
Park and Dare Unionist Club	0	10	0	Mr. Frape, Thistle Hotel, Tonypandy	0	7	0
Tydraw Colliery	7	9	6	Mr. W. H. Alexander, Colliers' Arms Hotel, Trealaw	2	0	0
Mr. C. Davies, Pandy Hotel, Tonypandy	1	7	6	Mr. Palmer Griffiths	1	4	0
Mr. D. Jones	0	0	6	Penygraig Conservative Club	0	4	0
Mr. J. Williams, Ynyswen	2	5	0	Mr. W. J. Morris, Butchers' Arms Hotel, Penygraig	3	17	0
County Club, Tonypandy	1	10	0	Mr. J. Brown, Silver Hotel, Gelli	0	11	0
Tylorstown Conservative Club	1	2	0	Mr. Dan Armstrong, Tonypandy	1	2	0
Mr. T. Roberts, Royal Hotel, Blaenclydach	2	9	6	Mr. Dai Price	1	8	0
Mr. Lewis Williams, Penygraig	2	16	0	Llwynypia Conservative Club	1	13	6
Do. do. do.	1	14	0	Mr. D. Davies, Ynyshir	0	17	6
Baden-Powell Conservative Club, Ynyshir	1	0	0	Maindy Conservative Club	0	7	0
Mr. W. John, Gethin Hotel, Penygraig	0	11	6	Mr. Dan Charles, Tonypandy	3	5	0
Treorchy Social Club	0	16	0	Hibernia Club Tonypandy	2	7	6
Clydach Vale Conservative Club	1	6	0	Mr. Davies, Ynyscynon Hotel	0	6	6
Llwynypia Fife Band Institute	0	19	0	Ton-Pentre Labour Club	0	8	0
Cardiff Park Conservative Club	1	1	0				
Mr. Jack Jones, Llwynypia	1	14	0				
Do. do. do.	0	1	6				
Treherbert Conservative Club	0	11	6				
Mr. W. Weston, Tonypandy	1	5	0				

Just some of the names of those that bought tickets

were, their enduring popularity and the care and affection shown by so many people.

Several years later in March 1916, while reminiscing with Matt Wells, Frank Torreyson revealed the class of fighters that Dai and Leslie were up against in choosing who to bring to America. "The selection was made from the following boxers: Ted Lewis, the now famous welterweight, boxing so sensationally in this country: Eddie Morgan, the featherweight, also doing so well around New York and the East: Fred Dyer, the great baritone singer and boxer who is about to invade this country from Australia, where he has done great work in the ring, only losing one bout, that to the sensational Darcy, and Fred Delaney, another welterweight, now doing well in Australia. Jimmy Wilde, who is now paperweight champion of England and holder of the Lonsdale belt of that class, was also offered, but was declined on account of his light weight, he only weighed ninety pounds. These two boys being selected from the above talent on account of their better showing must have been near champions."

Torreyson passed away two years later from pneumonia, just hours after his twenty nine year old son Clyde was laid to rest with the same affliction. Torreyson was too ill to attend his son's funeral. While the body of Leslie was pulled from the water and as if in exchange for his identification, being returned back to the Atlantic, Bowen had a different ending. In Treorchy Cemetery lies the grave of Dai's mother, and written underneath her name, "David John Bowen, who lost his life on the S.S. *Titanic* April 15 1912, aged 20 years. At Rest."

SOURCES & ACKNOWLEDGEMENTS

The Baltimore Sun (Baltimore, Maryland) - "Sporting Miscellany," Fri, Feb 2nd, 1906. Mon, Dec 14th, 1908. "Steamers To Sail From New York," Mon, Apr 8th, 1912. "Williams Welsh Bantam," Wed, Apr 24th, 1912.

The Philadelphia Inquirer (Philadelphia, Pennsylvania) - "In The Boxers' Corner," Sun, Nov 3rd, 1907. "McFarland And Welch Matched," Thu, Dec 3rd, 1908. Fri, Dec 4th, 1908. "Matt Wells Wins Title On Points," Tue, Feb 28th, 1911.

The Boston Globe (Boston, Massachusetts) - Tue, Dec 10th, 1907. Thu, Oct 5th, 1911. "Slowly Going Toward Halifax," Mon, Apr 15th, 1912. "Absolutely Unsinkable," Mon, Apr 15th, 1912. "Early Story Of Wreck," Mon, Apr 15th, 1912. "Just After *Titanic's* Launch," Tue, Apr 16th, 1912. "In Charge Of Services," Wed, Apr 24th, 1912. Wed, May 1st, 1912. "Chaplain Of The Mackay-Bennett," Wed, May 1st, 1912.

The Butte Daily Post (Butte, Montana) - "Driscoll Is Coming Over," Sat, Dec 21st, 1907.

The Stark County Democrat (Canton, Ohio) - "Driscoll Made Marto Look Foolish," Thu, Feb 4th, 1909.

Wilkes-Barre Times Leader (Wilkes-Barre, Pennsylvania) - "Owen Moran Is After Abe Attell," Mon, Mar 1st, 1909. "Fighters Coming Here Drowned In *Titanic* Wreck," Wed, Apr 24th, 1912.

Evening Express (Wales) - Mon, Jan 17th, 1910. "Champions of the Ring," Tue, Mar 15th, 1910. "Success of the Nazareth Assault-at-Arms," Thu, Mar 17th, 1910. Wed, Mar 30th, 1910. "Boxing - Knocked Out In Second Round," Mon, Apr 4th, 1910. "Boxing," Fri, Jul 1st, 1910. "Boxing Contest At Pontypridd," Tue, Jul 5th, 1910. "Fine Contest At Pentre," Fri, Aug 19th, 1910. "The Pentre Fight," Sat, Aug 20th, 1910. "Interesting Match," Wed, Sept 14th, 1910. "Monday's Interesting Fight," Fri, Oct 28th, 1910. "Challenge from Treherbert," Sat, Oct 29th, 1910. "Welsh Bantam Honours," Mon, Oct 31st, 1910. "Fight Stopped," Tue, Nov 1st, 1910. "Grainger's Winnings In The Pontypridd Match," Wed, Nov 2nd, 1910. "Reply to Dai Bowen," Thu, Nov 3rd, 1910. "Plain and Pat," Sat, Nov 5th, 1910. "Challenge to Dai Bowen," Mon, Nov 7th, 1910. "Challenge Accepted," Wed, Nov 30th, 1910.

The Morning Post (Camden, New Jersey) - Thu, Jan 27th, 1910.

Rhondda Leader Maesteg Garw And Ogmore Telegraph (Wales) - "Boxing Matinee at Tonypandy Empire," Sat, May 14th, 1910. "Assault-at-Arms at Pentre. Bowen Retains Prestige. A Hard Fight," Sat, Aug 27th, 1910. Sat, May 4th, 1912.

Evansville Press (Evansville, Indiana) - "By Pat," Mon, Jun 13th, 1910.

The Inter Ocean (Chicago, Illinois) - Sun, Nov 20th, 1910. "McFarland-Attell Battle Looks To Be Very, Very Far Away," Fri, Dec 16th, 1910.

The San Francisco Call (San Francisco, California) - "Abe Attell to Fight Packey McFarland," (Special Dispatch to The Call), Mon, Dec 5th, 1910. "$2,000 Posted To Insure Big Bout," Sun, Apr 21st, 1912.

The Rhondda Leader (Wales) - "Boxing Tragedy at Treherbert," Sat, Feb 4th, 1911. "The Value of an Agreement," Sat, Mar 11th, 1911. "Municipal Notes," Sat, Mar 18th, 1911. "Boxing Contests At Old Hippodrome," Sat, Mar 18th, 1911. Sat, Sep 23rd, 1911. "Assault-at-Arms at Pentre," Sat, Feb 17th, 1912. "The Awful Ocean

Tragedy," Sat, Apr 20th, 1912. "Local Victims of the *Titanic* Disaster," Sat, Apr 27th, 1912. "Gymkhana and Assault-at-Arms," Sat, May 4th, 1912. "A Record of the Historic *Titanic* Tragedy," Sat, May 4th, 1912. "Porth Palace," Sat, May 11th, 1912. "Porth," Sat, May 11th, 1912. "*Titanic* Relief Fund," Sat, May 18th, 1912. "Rhondda *Titanic* Relief Committee," Sat, May 18th, 1912. "Rhondda *Titanic* Benefit," Sat, Jun 8th, 1912. "Grand Mounted Military Tournament," Sat, Jun 15th, 1912. "*Titanic* Gymkhana and Assault-at-Arms at Tonypandy," Sat, Jun 29th, 1912. "Rhondda *Titanic* Benefit," Sat, Jul 13th, 1912. "Rhondda *Titanic* Benefit," Sat, Aug 31st, 1912. "Rhondda *Titanic* Benefit Fund," Sat, Aug 31st, 1912. "Balance Sheet and Details of Revenue," Sat, Sep 7th, 1912. "Rhondda *Titanic* Benefit," Sat, Sept 14th, 1912. "Rhondda *Titanic* Benefit, Appointment of Trustees," Sat, Sep 21st, 1912.

The Guardian (London, England) - "The Lightweight Championship," Tue, Feb 28th, 1911.

The Daily Times (Davenport, Iowa) - "Packy Wants Mac To Raise The Purse," Mon, Mar 6th, 1911.

Star Tribune (Minneapolis, Minnesota) - "Driscoll's Sparring Partner A Star," Mon, Mar 20th, 1911. "How *Titanic* Was Destroyed," Fri, Apr

19th, 1912. "*Titanic's* People Calm Following Awful Collision," Fri, Apr 19th, 1912.

The Washington Post (Washington, District of Columbia) - Fir, May 19th, 1911. Sun, Dec 15th, 1912.

Bisbee Daily Review (Bisbee, Arizona) - "With The Boxers," Wed, Oct 11th, 1911.

San Francisco Chronicle (San Francisco, California) - Tue, Oct 24th, 1911.

The Tribune-Republican (Scranton, Pennsylvania) - "Fighter Meets Boxer: Quit With Honors Even," Sat, Mar 16th, 1912. "Third Cabin," Thu, Apr 18th, 1912. "Two Welsh Boxers Die On *Titanic*," Wed, Apr 24th, 1912. "Howells Believes His Friends Were Drowned," Wed, Apr 24th, 1912.

Calgary Herald (Calgary, Alberta, Canada) - "*Titanic* Completed," Wed, Apr 3rd, 1912.

Coshocton Daily Age (Coshocton, Ohio) - "*Titanic* Makes Maiden Voyage," Mon, Apr 8th, 1912.

The Evening World (New York, New York) - "Big Liner *Titanic* Upsets Harbor On Her First Trip Out," Wed, Apr 10th, 1912.

The Marion Star (Marion, Ohio) - "*Titanic* Sails On First Trip," Wed, Apr 10th, 1912.

The Evening Sun (Baltimore, Maryland) - "*Titanic* In Peril On Maiden Voyage," Thu, Apr 11th, 1912.

Pittsburgh Post-Gazette (Pittsburgh, Pennsylvania) - Tue, Apr 16th, 1912. "Fighter's Body Buried at Sea," Sun, May 5th, 1912. Sun, Oct 29th, 1916.

Stevens Point Journal (Stevens Point, Wisconsin) - "*Titanic* Sinks; 1490 Drowned; 866 Are Saved," Tue, Apr 16th, 1912.

The Washington Herald (Washington, District of Columbia) - "The World Mourns," Tue, Apr 16th, 1912.

The Brooklyn Daily Eagle (Brooklyn, New York) - "Third Class Passengers," Wed, Apr 17th, 1912. "Bodies Identified From White Star Passenger List," Tue, Apr 23rd, 1912.

The Alexandria Times-Tribune (Alexandria, Indiana) - "Pugs Probably Lost," Thu, Apr 18th, 1912.

The Buffalo Enquirer (Buffalo, New York) - "Boxers Drowned," Thu, Apr 18th, 1912.

Salt Lake Telegram (Salt Lake City, Utah) - "Supreme Faith In Great Vessel Cost Many Lives," Fri, Apr 19th, 1912.

Quad-City Times (Davenport, Iowa) - "Pugilist Dies On Steamer *Titanic*," Fri, Apr 19th, 1912.

The News (Paterson, New Jersey) - "Two English Boxers Perish," Sat, Apr 20th, 1912.

Pittsburgh Daily Post (Pittsburgh, Pennsylvania) - Sat, Apr 20th, 1912. "Frank Torreyson And Wife Are Ill; Can't Attend Son's Funeral Today," Wed, Apr 10th, 1918. "Frank Torreyson Dies, Following Son Closely," Thu, Apr 11th, 1918.

The Times (Munster, Indiana) - "Two Boxers Die On *Titanic*," Sat, Apr 20th, 1912.

The Buffalo Commercial (Buffalo, New York) - "Boxers on *Titanic*," Tue, Apr 23rd, 1912.

The Star Press (Muncie, Indiana) - "Pugilist Among Lost in *Titanic* Disaster," Wed, Apr 24th, 1912.

The Gazette (York, Pennsylvania) - "Heard Breaking Up Signs," Wed, Apr 24th, 1912.

Pittston Gazette (Pittston, Pennsylvania) - "Welsh Boxers Among The *Titanic's* Victims," Wed, Apr 24th, 1912. "Notes And Comment On Sporting Events," Tue, Jul 30th, 1912.

The Scranton Truth (Scranton, Pennsylvania) - "Welsh Boxers Among Victims," Wed, Apr 24th, 1912. Tue, Dec 31st, 1912.

The Evening News (Wilkes-Barre, Pennsylvania) - "Scranton Fighter's Funeral," Thu, Apr 25th, 1912.

The Hope Pioneer (Hope, North Dakota) - Thu, Apr 25th, 1912.

Neodesha Register (Neodesha, Kansas) - "*Titanic* Immediately After Launching," Thu, Apr 25th, 1912.

The Windsor Star (Windsor, Ontario) - "Welsh Bantam Fighter Was *Titanic* Victim," Fri,

Apr 26th, 1912.

The Ogden Standard (Ogden, Utah) - "Packey Had A Big Cinch," Sat, Apr 27th, 1912. Thu, Feb 13th, 1913.

The Gazette (Cedar Rapids, Iowa) - Sat, Apr 27th, 1912.

Lincoln Journal Star (Lincoln, Nebraska) - "Captain Tells Graphic Story," Tue, Apr 30th, 1912.

Buffalo Evening News (Buffalo, New York) - Tue, Apr 30th, 1912.

Chicago Tribune (Chicago, Illinois) - "Packey Returns; Wants Wolgast," Wed, May 1st, 1912.

The Daily Republican (Rushville, Indiana) - "The Wreck Of The Titan," Wed, May 1st, 1912.

The Winnipeg Tribune (Winnipeg, Manitoba, Canada) - "Charlie Lucca," Thu, May 2nd, 1912.

The Tennessean (Nashville, Tennessee) - "Many Victims Of Ocean Disaster Buried In Halifax," Sat, May 4th, 1912.

St. Louis Post-Dispatch (St. Louis, Missouri) - Sun, Jun 23rd, 1912.

The Cincinnati Enquirer (Cincinnati, Ohio) - Sun, Jun 23rd, 1912. Sun, Mar 26th, 1916.

The Pittsburgh Press (Pittsburgh, Pennsylvania) - "By Jim Jab," Mon, Aug 12th, 1912.

Evening Star (Washington, District of Columbia) - Sun, Sep 1st, 1912.

The Buffalo Times (Buffalo, New York) - Tue, Nov 12th, 1912.

Oakland Tribune (Oakland, California) - "Welsh And Wells Go Causes Difference Of Opinions," Sun, Nov 24th, 1912.

The Marshfield News and Wisconsin Hub (Marshfield, Wisconsin) - "Matt Wells, Ex-Boxer, Makes Hit As Referee," Thu, Mar 7th, 1918.

Websites used: Newspapers.Library.Wales, Newspapers.com, Ancestry.co.uk, Findmypast.co.uk, Encyclopedia-Titanic.org, NovaScotia.ca/archives, Britishnewspaperarchive.co.uk.

I would also like to say a special thank you to a few people. Steve Compton, boxing historian and author, who first told me I should write this book myself and who directed me to the University of Notre Dame, telling me they held in their archives some old 'Boxing' publications. Without this encouragement, I would not have been able to do this. Tad Fitch, *Titanic* historian and author, who took the time to read over several sections I wrote and for opening my mind to the realisation of what faced the passengers. Douglas Cavanaugh, boxing historian and author and a real inspiration to me. Nobody knows Pittsburgh boxing like Douglas knows Pittsburgh boxing, and nobody spends as much of their time on the history of the Steel City fighters and their legacies. Harley Dallison, who I talk to every other day about boxing and who looked over some of my writing as I was going along. Thank you for continually supporting me and giving me the confidence to do this. Darren Pullman, for visiting the grave of Dai and sending me incredible pictures of this and of Dai and Leslie's childhood homes. Radoslav Metodiev of Sports Wallpaper, a big thank you for taking the time to produce my book cover. Springs Toledo, boxing historian and author whose writing is continually praised and who was kind enough to read over parts of my book and give me invaluable feedback. James Cachey and Debra Dochuk of the Rare Books & Special Collections department, University of Notre Dame, for searching the archives and sending me the weekly 'Boxing' publications. Stewart Gillies, News Reference Team Leader for The British Library, for sending me the weekly 'Boxing' publications. Jessica Kilford, Photograph Technician for the Nova Scotia Archives, for taking the time to send me information about the *Titanic* victims and for granting me the authority to use such pictures supplied on their site. Lastly, Lyubo Mihailov. I met Lyubo several years ago through social media and our mutual interest in boxing history meant an instant connection. Without our friendship, I have no doubt this book would still be an idea in my mind. I can't place a value on our friendship and all the late night and early morning conversations we have on boxing. I thank you Lyubo.

Printed in Great Britain
by Amazon